AF545195

Fairytales and Sail Boats

Ride the waves of imagination

To and from the sun

The journey is heavenly and fun

WELCOME TO

Pieces of JIMMY

JIMMY D. ROBINSON

Musical Stories, Lyrics, Songs, Poetry

Strawberries Heal Wounds

She's My Star

She's Giggling

Music Is Life

JIMMY

GRAVES OF HEAVEN

Wisdom, Sailboats and Screams

WITHOUT YOU

SOUND PROOF

A PLUM WEEPS

Music And Fairytales

Carry Our Love

Music Factory

SOLDIERS

Message of Beauty

THE CRICKETS

Moon Swept Fear

Ghosts in his heaven

She Was There

Pillow Songs

PEEKS OF DAWN

TIDES of COLOR

ONE CHANCE

The Moon Is Lying

MOMENTS OF PEACE

Like Toasted Cherries

Just Like

Pillow Songs II

And In Time

People are People

Guide the Ship

One Rose

PRISON LIFE

Strawberries Heal Wounds

In all my thought...
Emotions get caught in all of my day

Apples and cherries grow Happily always
May Love enter your Soul
May guidance take its toll

As I walk, sounds of Laughter spark the air
an elephant giggles tip toes
And stares at all the children of the world.

Cries pour out of clouds for
Harmony to sweep this earths land
More cries cover the sand

Music is finally at last bringing
Unity to this great Land

Come Together... Come Together
Strawberries heal wounds...
And the moon drips
The music that brings peace to the world

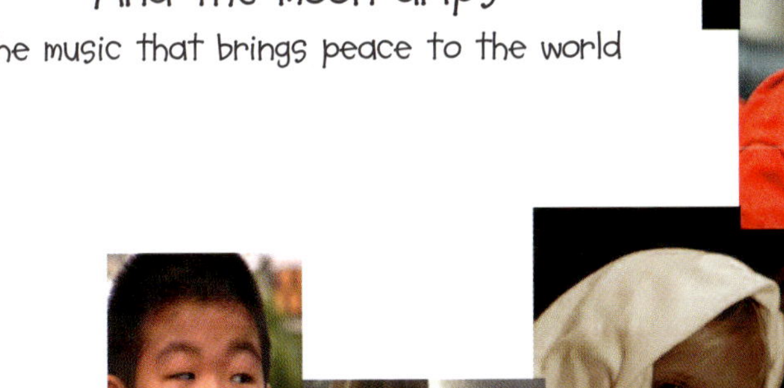

She's My Star

She took me into her arms
She made me see the rainbows in my life
Yeah
It was a struggle at first
But; I finally opened my eyes after many, many falls . . .

I realized she was there guiding my light toward the sunshine
I thought the ghosts at night brought my soul peace
But I realize imagination came alive during the day
Like when the tulips bloom and the cherry blossoms . . .
Brought music to my song

I would walk . . .
And soldiers would guard my way pushing me to stop crying
I was really, really crying

But my Fairy Princess would use her wisdom and light
To Guide my soul towards its innermost strength

Which is Love

The dreams came alive during the day as helicopters took me away . . .
As the stars were my ships my mystery ship . . .
Which sailed me towards the sun
As I became the star...

My Soul of Love Finally Won

She's Giggling

She's giggling at the musical show and
Giving her all to the people who watch her glow
But, inside she is desperately trying to unravel the smoke...
So she too can enjoy the world of love
The world of Love
Which I sometimes foolishly blow into the fires...

The forest is burning at her delight waiting and waiting
For her love to cherish the color in the sunlight

Yeah! She is Me, and we could conquer and explore together

If she would just open her eyes and stop stealing the raindrops...
Which Shine in My eyes

Give me the chance...
And then the Love that you want to feel...
Will come to You
Because I'm the Sunshine of Your Life...

Music Is Life

Music brings life and color to this Land.
I don't think anyone can quite understand the glow
That music brings to this Earth's sand . . .

Madonna and Jimmy

Understand their Souls go hand and hand . . .
Their music and dance sweep this Neverland
Mystery and Intrigue is what the earth gets out of their Hands
It's a Musical Wonderland

Tiptoeing through clouds go color of intrigue
Into Minds . . . Yes, Indeed
This is something that all people of the world need
They read . . . We plant the seed
It's an Explosive combination which Blows through
The Musical Wonderland and lands in the sand . . .

Composers and musicians

Both want to experience this Magical Hand
But through God only two on the planet really can. But . . .
Through Love and Music you too can enter this wonderland and
Feel the Magic and Glow

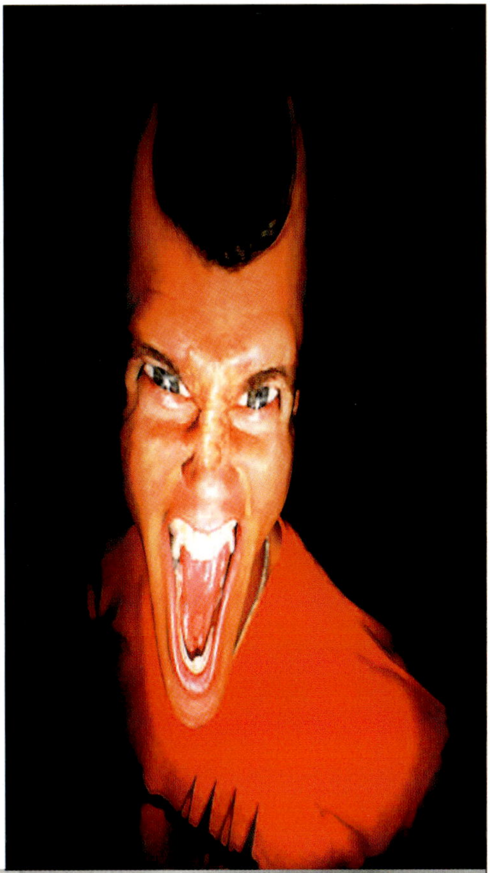

My eyes have seen everything
From the coasts to the mountains
To the cities . . . to digging potatoes
What a Life
Some beautiful days, some filled with strife
But through it all I seem to survive
Through all these walls which surround Me . . .
Always will I be just . . .

Jimmy

Cries have seen my eyes
Lies have taken me to the sky
Happiness comes with Love
And as I walk new days come with . . .
The rising of the sun
This journey is Heavenly and Fun
This journey to the moon . . . that is . . .
I'm learning the fun . . . is in the trip
And as I continue to seek
All the Happiness shall I Reap
With Love I shall only grow
And as I near my End
I WILL BE MY ONLY FRIEND
And the message I send
To Everyone
Is Free
Your Soul from Within

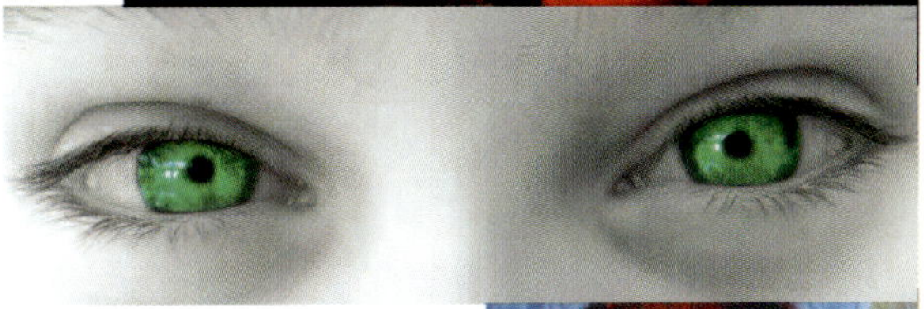

GRAVES OF HEAVEN

I Start to touch her and rose petals come to life
As the morning sends messages of love
I capture her heart and all the poison is shed
From days gone by that were filled with pain
It's like rose petals came up from the graves of heaven
To wash My eyes

Pieces of my touch which guide us through the storms
Which guide us through the poisonous thorns
Which touched sleeping eyes
I awoke through tears of pain
And was guided by rose petals above the graves of wicked Smiles

As I run into tomorrows I run into the wounds of yesterday
But I trust my heart and capture the need to dance...
To the tone of tomorrow's flight

As tomorrow guides my journey as rose petals sing always in this life . . .

NOBODY *gets because the world is crying*

As my tears fall through the mountains

NOBODY *gets pain because drifting to the ocean floors are sorrows . . .*

Heaven knows if you change your life butterflies will…

Spoiled thought turns the fruits of life into colorful nights..

Thanks for the piece of history Sir!

AS THE JUICES FLOW DEVILISH THOUGHT TIP TOES…

Soundproof is the wine be sure to drink 100 years after its time

Because if you do your soul will be ripened . . .

Finally, many, many thoughts mixed with grapes

Cause the years of my life to celebrate,

As Jimmy's art flows

SOUND PROOF

Wisdom, Sailboats and Screams

THEY want me to digest their thought

Their realms of whatever
But entailed in this dream is only my wisdom
And by chance
if I Fall into your sunlight
May we ride the waves of oceans together

May our dreams entwine...
But I shall follow my path of heaven
And love and guidance from white doves
And dancing in endless dreams of

Wisdom, Sailboats and Screams
And tides of endless dreams

My story is easy...
as I walk the brick streets of willow trees
And writing my song which stroke the wings of **white doves...**
And may the waves of mellowness mend my leaves
As I dance to the greatness of endless dreams of...

Wisdom, Sailboats and Screams

And tides of endless dreams

Music And Fairytales

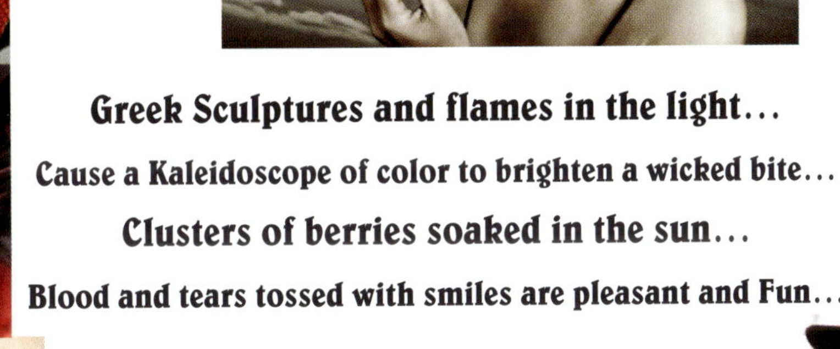

Greek Sculptures and flames in the light...
Cause a Kaleidoscope of color to brighten a wicked bite...
Clusters of berries soaked in the sun...
Blood and tears tossed with smiles are pleasant and Fun...

On top of rainbows are tides of thought...
It's a Forbidden World it is...

Lost times and memories gone astray...
Bitter wounds of terror feel nothing...
But if the frozen thought opens their eyes and captures
The Need to dance to the endless trance of 40,000 years of Dance;
Then freedom will...

Then freedom will replenish of bittersweet....
And cherry blossoms will stroll the sun drenched streets of endless...

Music And Fairytales

As the Drums Beat the Fires

An Indian boy embeds a Flame of Light in the forest
Sunshine guides the journey
Love and Darkness Have Touched His Soul
Diamonds have split Thorns at his Feet
Change is Needed
Justice is Greeted
But Joy has come after his flight to the mountains
His Eyes touched the tombs of many Souls
Shredded were his Roots
But history touched this land
As the Indian Boy Guided all his People to the Promise Land
Sweat and Tears Roam Free
An Eagle Soars toward the sun
The Boy is Home at last
As a Sword touches his soul
Shedded Tears bring Justice to the Land
The Free explore Forbidden ground
Inside the Graves of Man...
... The Boy is Free..
A Plum Sucks the Juices from
The Land of the Free

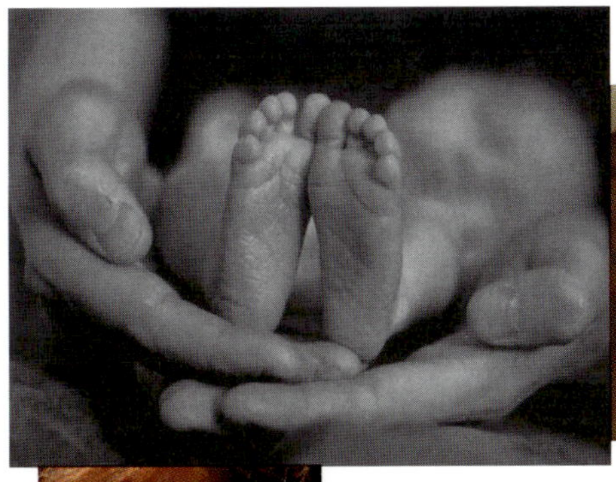

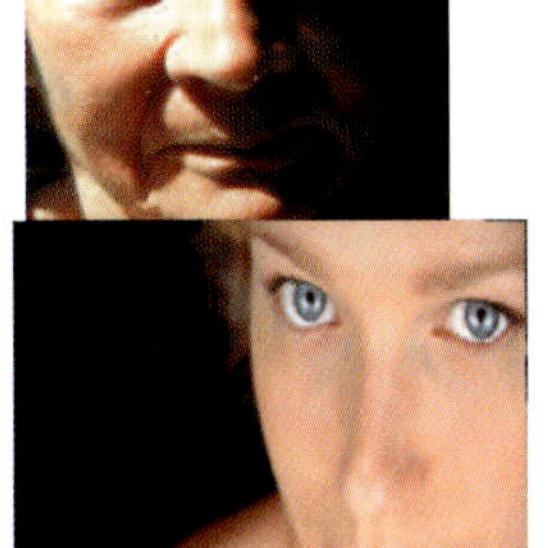

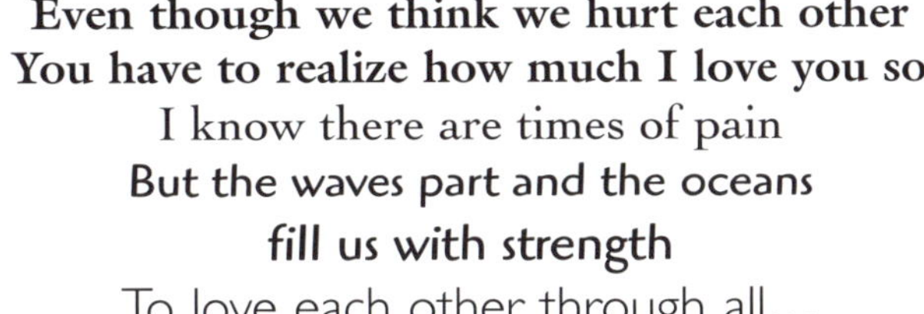

Even though we think we hurt each other
You have to realize how much I love you so
I know there are times of pain
But the waves part and the oceans
fill us with strength
To love each other through all…

<u>I can't imagine life without you</u>

Because you are so SPECIAL

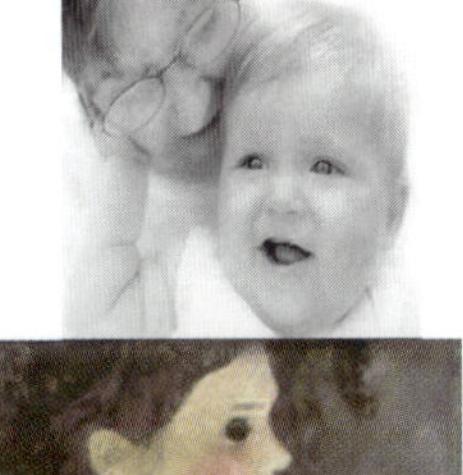

There's only one of you in this
lifetime
Yes, only one in this lifetime

If you go my heart will never mend…
And the pain will drive my tears
into the oceans forever

But understand I LOVE YOU so,

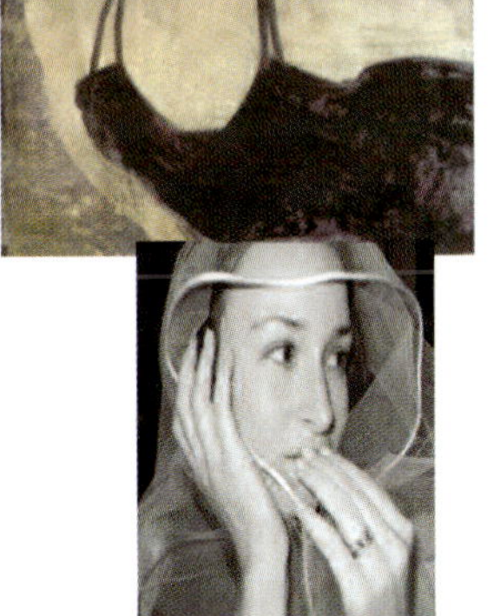

I want you to know if there
comes a day like tomorrow…
Then I'll run with you through all the tulips
And touch your smiles forever

Please Realize

I can't imagine life without you

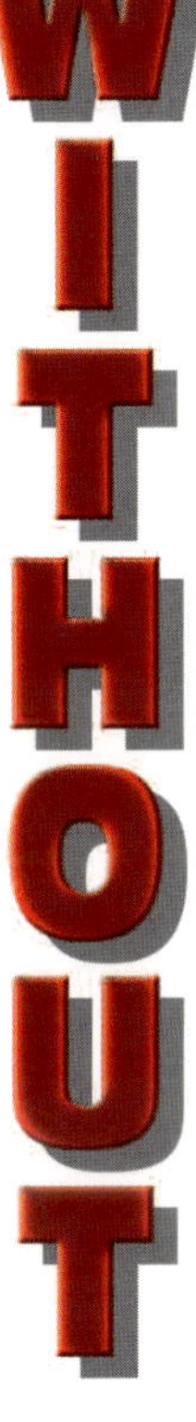

WITHOUT YOU

There is a Mist in the Wind...

As the Blueness in the Sky Touches

The Soul of Peace...

The marching of the guard

Sets a New Light after the children Tiptoe...

Songs are the Music as we gather and Start Life

The Journey is short so enjoy the Pleasure

The plums search inside for realms of Love

Drums beat in the forest

A flicker of Light sheds the Pain of a million years

Of being Insane.

But guarded is the future as time

Sheds the sunlight...

And the children digest the fruits of beautiful smiles.

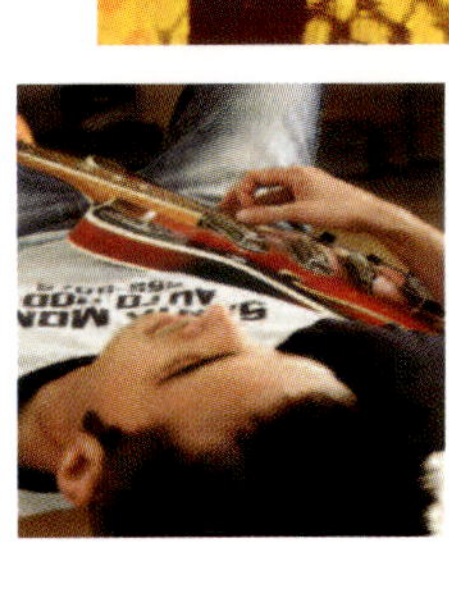

Latin men bring together in the trees "LOVE"

Lips embed the Joy...

The brothers and sisters make the journey Wild

Plums suck their feet

God touches their soul

And brings them peace towards each other.

As the sunlight guides them

To the Promised Land where

The Plums Rule Forever

Message of Beauty

AROUND MY EYES IS A GLOW
THAT RAINS BEAUTIFULLY SO.
Throughout the day and every day with the breeze
Comes the beauty from within.
Its texture is like no other
In the world we flavor to see.
A PICTURE OF TOGETHERNESS IS ALWAYS
WHAT WE STRIVE TO BE.
But in order to reach this I must
First free myself from all the
People that roam this land with a sword in hand.
LET THEIR MOVEMENT FADE AWAY
Let their darkness stay under the bridges
Where all the grayness is able to stay.
Let the message of beauty always come my way
Let the chariots carry me up through the gray
Let the message always hold my thoughts
For me to share with the heavens
On my golden day.
LET THE LOVE BE STILL
MOMENTS OF BEAUTY ARE THE THRILL
Take my soul to the place
To the land of the grace
Where the diamonds rule.
Always keep the message
of **BEAUTY ON MY FACE**
To share with the world
As one with the human race.

Moon Swept Fear

Moon swept fear is creepy
Because up above the ominous clouds
A Light is trying to infuse a good day
Scatter the bones in the
Graves of time . . .
Skeletons are a Smile in the Music I mold
Tears on my shoulder are Rivers
In my Soul. . .
If I had You closer . . .
Alone, but Gone . . .
A Star***
. . . a penny turned to Dust . . .
Just Emotions crying to hold you so . . .

Journey to the Wild where Creatures are Shining
Footsteps that Walk my feet like a lost
Stranger in the shallow waters of History
. . . Torture . . . A Band Of Symphony . . .
Reap a Hollow Mind . . . a tale untold . . .
Yesterday captures a sparrow
Climbing up a mountain Soaring
Toward the sky . . .
. . . A bell Chimes . . .
A hundred years or so . . .
. . . Backward and Forward to go . . .
Will it stop?
Will the Music burst?
Apple trees grow
Black cats tiptoe
Mend my leaves
Will it stop? Will the Music burst?
A stroke of genius
Eyes of Jimmy

Ghosts in his heaven

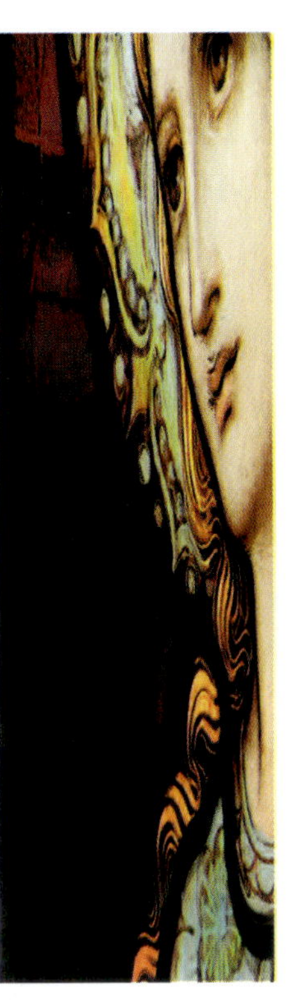

He's dreaming

And there are ghosts in his heaven . . .

Yeah, I don't know if they're cloudy

Or full of spirits

But I do know

The Ghosts are talking and singing in the night . . .

They're there! Yeah . . .

The ghosts are guiding his dreams and holding the sunlight

For the day when the ominous Feelings of pain fade away

Maybe they're pulling at the flowers . . .

The sunlight will guide the way

Yeah . . .

Imagine the ghosts playing in the sunlight . . .

And waking up with tulips in the air . . .

And realizing that all the visions are imaginary

And all the dreams of ghosts . . .

Weren't there

Carry Our Love

I get the feel of Loneliness
Sometimes I get the Feel of Her in my Heart
I just want to close my eyes and start...
Start the Dreams...
SLOWLY THE MUSIC COMES TO LIFE
I get the Feel of this in my Heart
To let the Stars Play
I just want to close my Eyes so I can Dream in the Wind
I just want to believe that butterflies
Will Mend my Pain...
I HAVE THE POWER
Sometimes I get the Feel of Her Heart
Touching painted Castles and playing
In the Sand...
As memories unlock my Heart
I look at the Moon
And you are there...
I look through the Stars and suddenly...
I have you in my arms forever...
Till the End when
Butterflies pick us up... And

To the Sky

FOREVER . . .

SOLDIERS

Persistent are the folks to take control of my life . . .

But determination and growth cause a
New revolution in my soul
The soldiers stand guard—
A New life begins to unfold,
The bodies of yesterday still rise with the sun…
But the new minds control the wisdom,
The joy and the peace…
All this good fortune rains in
The forest everyday.
On top of mountains not only grows is the green grass
But the Laughter of rains as well
The soldiers guard the light
As communication makes the sky
Turn a beautiful **blue**
It's alright to dream . . .
It's beautiful to let your heart scream . . .
Flowers will rain . . .
As tulips kiss the land
And all the world will glow . . .
Music is here . . . believe me . . .
The people will stare
As the star that shines
Everyday of the journey through life...

As Soldiers stand guard

Do you think that my dreams are just Painted pictures in the sky
Or
Pillow Songs in the tears of my cries?
Or is this just a time when ...
I have set myself higher above the storms
And above the rains of the night

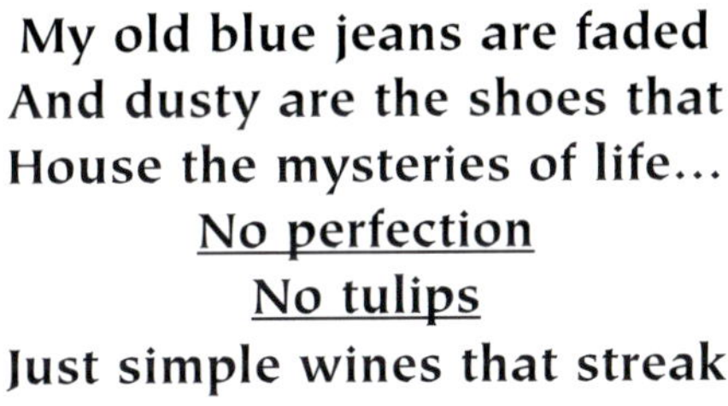

My old blue jeans are faded
And dusty are the shoes that
House the mysteries of life...
No perfection
No tulips
Just simple wines that streak

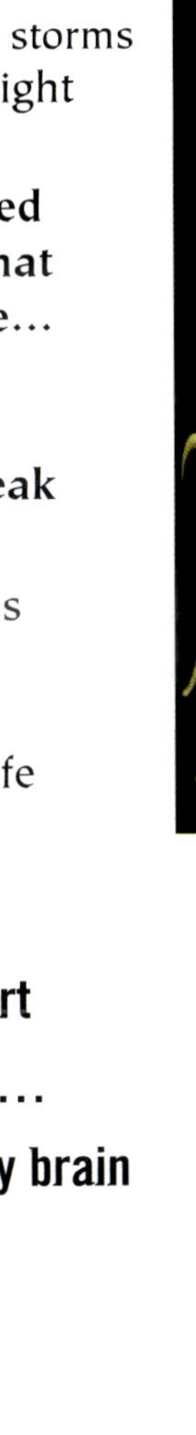

The forest of ancient times
an old record playing
Sweet, sweet candies...
It is the diamonds in my life

Need to change

So that the vein to my heart

Keeps stroking the wisdom...

That sails the Imagination to my brain

THE CRICKETS

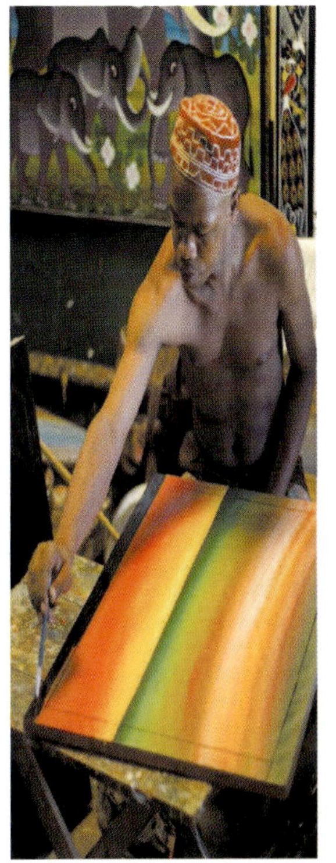

And I shall capture a star
That is falling from afar
And with it I shall carry the crickets
Into the night
And blossom with love is right . . .
And as we pressure our thought
It shall rekindle moments brought.
It shall bring all the crickets our way.
And as we start to grow
Good moments will come and go.
But through it all
Crickets will stand tall...
And when the rain falls from above,
It will capture the love that we hold.
And slowly the message will
Be for the crickets . . .

The crickets show us
Freedom in life always
During the night

And always sing the
Message that is right . . .

She Was There

There was this thief in the night,
Who was always tiptoeing in
My dreams...
She was there
But just a touch of her perfume
Scented the air... some of
The times, even wicked cats
Would stare
And wonder! Was she there?
Or was it just the imagination
In my thoughts!
Was she there to help?
Or was she tiptoeing through my screams...
Into my beats...
Into the music, that sang in my soul...
All I know is that she was there...
Staring and glowing
Like the sunshine
As her everlasting beat
Finally touched my
Electric feet...

PEEKS OF DAWN

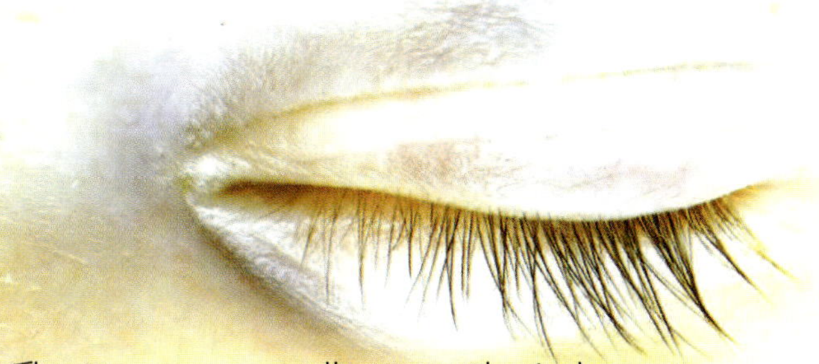

The tears were endless as the judgment

Day was near.

The kid was crying because his tears were
Fading
Into the dust...
The horizon peeked over the water's edge,
Life inside...
The dreams were gone...

His life was stolen... because the

Petals were melting inside his heart...
The judge was pending news of a life of misery...
Gates closed his eyes...
Chains were woven endlessly about...
Movement took him away to
Another realm...

Madness in thought...

But time stopped and the boy guided
His journey toward the sun
And out of his eyes were growing sunflowers...
Judgment day awaited trial
Forced confessions brought
Smiles and warmth...

He guided his soul toward the moon

And afterward
Love entered and life was

Endless at the peeks of dawn

MOMENTS OF PEACE

As we live and we are free all the brother and sisters you and me...
In this land of golden skies where
Sunlight comes with alibis
Rose petals all grow and to the
Soul we made the music just so,
Rose petals are to the light
As the song sounds alright...

Fire keeps trying to burn me
But I walk through it
The fire keeps coming
But I walk through and rainbows
Appear...

A NEW LIFE IS OVER THE HORIZON

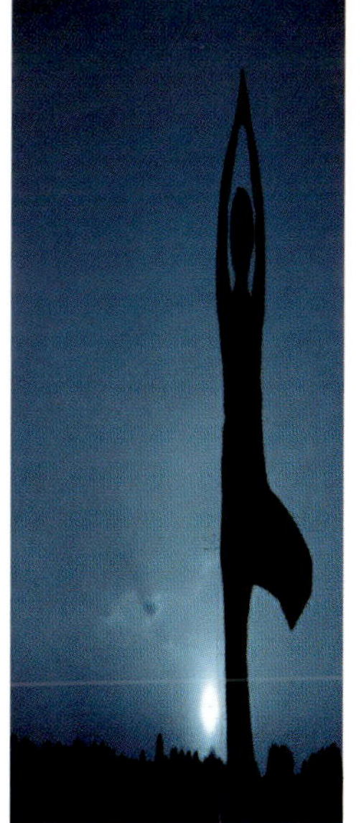

With sunshine and moments of peace
But the fires keep burning.
But my soul touches a new life
With honesty love and
Pieces of rose petals...
A new life sucks my soul
And the mountains bring me to
A song of peace...
As I walk through the fires
As peace tranquils the soul

AND LIFE BEGINS TO UNFOLD

The Moon Is Lying

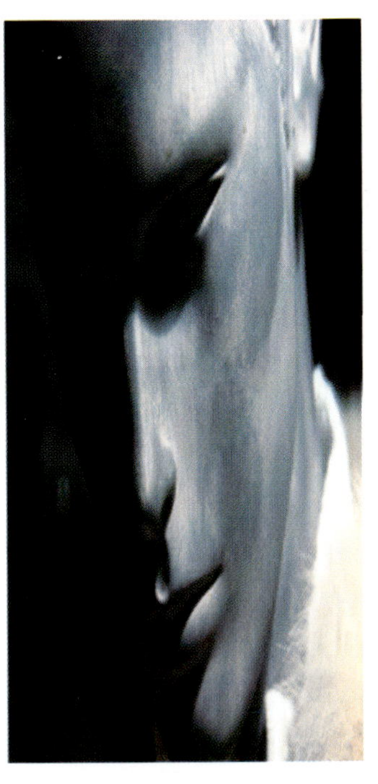

The moon is lying...
My tears are crying...
Morning is near
Before it appears twilight stars the night
Away into a cloud a diamond
Is calling for music to bring
The earth freedom...
Ships dance
A song is the romance
I need your love to take
My **footsteps and melt**
Them into an endless dream.
The moon is there
As my years bring a
Morning with peace
Rose petals grow and to
the light the music is always

Ruby lips and cherished
Dreams come into my life,
As the wisdom of morning
Songs dance with me on the
Moon…
I'm here and I'm afar
As the twilight of my love
Stokes the fires of desire…
Come and travel the roads
Of pleasant skies
As we turn this melody
Into simple lullabies of the
Music that sings deep inside of my heart

To further the songs that sing

In my heart.
One hand is not enough to
Enlighten the wisdom that
Dances with me in the dark.
As the wings of morning songs
Stroke the windows of captured
Stars…
One chance is not enough
To open my heart and let
The mellow softness of you fall into me

TIDES of COLOR

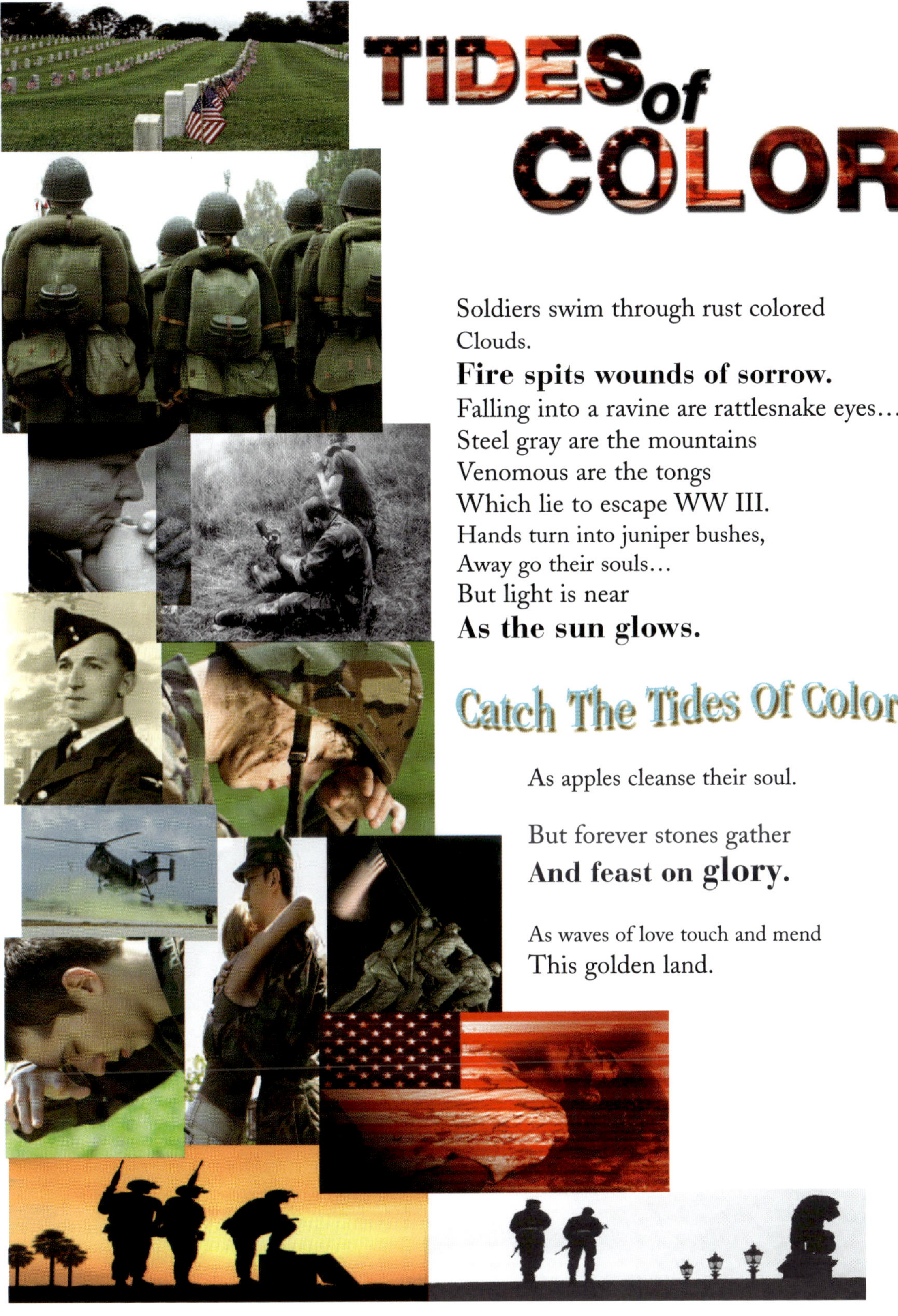

Soldiers swim through rust colored
Clouds.
Fire spits wounds of sorrow.
Falling into a ravine are rattlesnake eyes…
Steel gray are the mountains
Venomous are the tongs
Which lie to escape WW III.
Hands turn into juniper bushes,
Away go their souls…
But light is near
As the sun glows.

Catch The Tides Of Color

As apples cleanse their soul.

But forever stones gather
And feast on glory.

As waves of love touch and mend
This golden land.

Just Like

Just like the strawberries in a field of
Laughter tomorrow comes...

The music is the life inside of my heart.

So come here and let my hands
Wash away your tears... let the song
Of peace guide us above the song
Of loneliness...

My heart is just a pillow song in the
Night, touched by the stars that burn
Bright... waiting and waiting
For my happiness to touch the ray
Of color in the sunlight...

Yeah she is me and all my love
Is all I have to share with you

So come close and let the
Music of my heart fade away
All of loneliness
That rains inside of
The earth's tears...

Like Toasted Cherries

Like toasted cherries dancing on top
Of chimneys in the Wicked cool
Of the Night,
You're there inside of my dreams
Of shattered delight . . .
It's the imagination and laughter
That bring the ghosts alive
That melt the graves inside my
Raspberry eyes...
It's a memory gone astray . . .
OF ROAMING VILLAGES
WHERE BLACK CAT'S PLAY . . .

The festival of Music is pouring
Love on the Mountains . . .
DRAGONFLIES SING IN
BEATLES TIP TOE IN
SUNFLOWERS SWAYING
IN THE BREEZE . . .
As the bridges
of my Heart
Bring us unto
THE SONGS THAT SET US FREE

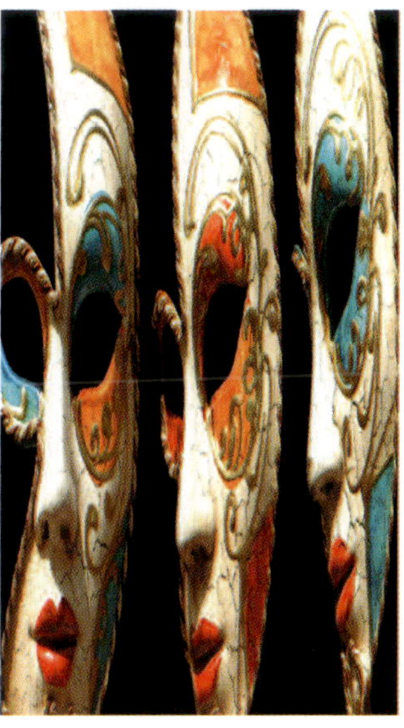

And In Time

And in time all my warmth
Will entwine my love...
And on this journey the mellow
Softness of your touch is endless
As evergreen
As the FOREST THAT BURNS BRIGHT
AS SUNLIGHT THAT CAPTURES MY THOUGHTS
Of imagination
And as the trees protect my
Wisdom
May the journey to the sun
Rain within my heart...
My melting heart which echos
Moments of laughter as well
As sunflowers blooming endlessly
Throughout my forest of love
As the trees of life sparkle
With magnificence
Of my hands and feet

Pillow Songs II

My old blue jeans are faded
And dusty are the shoes
That house, the mysteries of life...
No perfection... No tulips

Just simple wines that streak the forests
Of ancient times

And old record playing
Sweet, sweet candies...

Do you think my dreams
Are painted pictures in the sky
Or pillow songs in the tears of my cries

Guide the Ship

Fear of a forgotten land
Pain from yesterday inside of that Perfect flower won't seem to walk away…
Morning star Everything I hold for you
Even if the waves part the oceans will never sail us apart…
I can't imagine life without you
Guide the ship from steel gray rattlesnake eyes
Always through my walk…
Even though A symphony of sunlight…
Just a touch from my heart
<u>Must never let you go…</u>
Inescapable your hand soaring with my tear drops,
Torture and despair of days gone by…
Yesterday darkness seemingly Unforgettable
Stumbles fallen down a mountain Into walls of hell…
A shadow trying to escape 40,000 years of dance…
Blanket of fire searches
To take that Perfect flower…
Darken its petals Wilt the eyes of happiness
Shake the branches of time…
<u>Never let go</u>
Make the soul and body free To explore music…
Make the vein of evil Close its eyes
AND FADE AWAY INTO

The Graves of Dust…

People are People

I'm melting away
If I could just touch your heart
This dream would come alive…

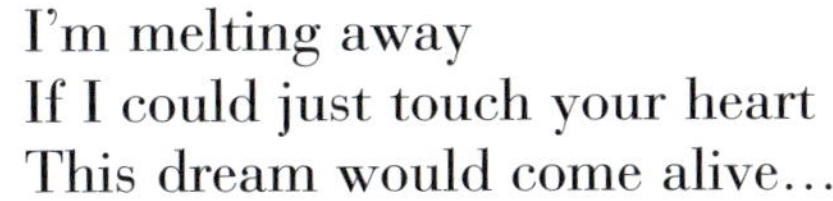

Like magic, magic mountain
Where a castle is lost in a song…

A parade of dancers…
The glory…

PEOPLE ARE PEOPLE
On this earth…

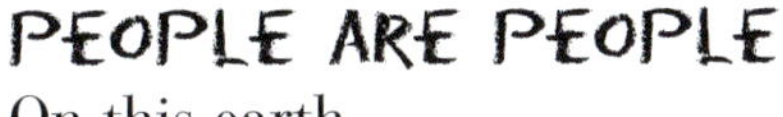

SO LET THE MUSIC BEGIN
Sorry isn't the answer and the tears won't go away…
Unless you change your life…

Ride a wave … walk or follow the moon
But do it soon because…

People are people . . .
Unless you open your heart it will
ALL FADE AWAY INTO A LIE
So just realize

People are people
So make this dream
Come pouring down
Out of a blue sky…

PRISON LIFE

Prison life what a mysterious game
Complex minds living life like the mentally insane
Difference of opinion hoping to change
Trying desperately to escape the manipulative game
Much of prison life is all the same
Connections mind direction
Having dinner at the same time

Part of a game

Believe it or not, all this crap is a whirlwind of the lame
But if you reach out and try to move through the gates

MAKE SURE YOU HEAD TOWARDS THE MOON

Your destiny will explode
Love will enter your body soon
Make a new life
With visibility and nice . . .
Then you just might reach the moon . . .

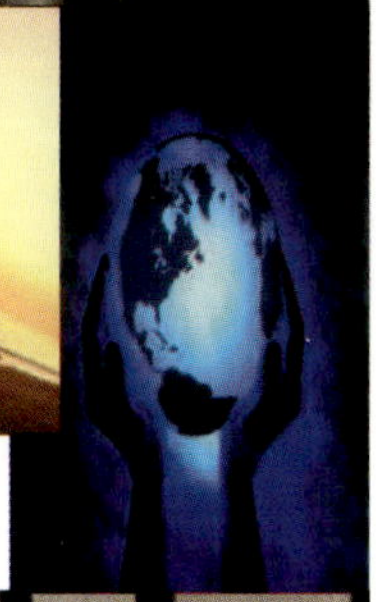

Get rid of the extravagant life
Especially if it's going to cost you your time

MAKE AN HONEST LIFE

With children, love and nice...
Give job action time to make all life's possibilities part of you . . .
Reach out touch honesty and love

Give your new life a chance
If you do you'll make to the moon tonight . . .
Your life will be out of sight
And your children will grow with love and right . . .

You'll make it to the moon tonight

One Rose

Why CAN'T I JUST HELP
THE ONE ROSE THAT ENLIGHTENED MY HEART?

Why can't I help the one rose follow its dreams
Can I feel the rose crying in the rain?
Can I see its petals melting into the ocean waves
Can I or does my heart follow a thorn?

A whisper
A teardrop
A penny in the dust

Where would I be without that
Rose **close by...**
Like a mirror...

See ghosts staring at me

Hoping and praying that
I'll take that rose and
Guide its journey to freedom...

Toward the sun...

As the truth sets me free.

THE END

Love,
Jimmy

Library of Congress Cataloging in Publication Data

Robinson, D. Jimmy

Pieces of Jimmy: musical stories, lyrics, songs, poetry—1st ed.
Jimmyland Corporation

ISBN: 0-9760140-0-9

Printed in the United States of America

Acknowledgments

This book has been made possible through the efforts of several people who have contributed directly to it and those who have inspired me and supported me through the years.

I would like to thank Victoria Marchant for her extraordinary talents, her endless hours, and patience throughout the project. To Johnny Varela, for being my source of inspiration—he continues to fill me with ideas and good thought. To Peter Keil, my good friend, for believing in me and helping me realize my dreams—and to his family Bo, Benjamin, Dennis, Kevin, and Jasmine.

To Betty Marcus for standing by me. Thank you for being such a good friend and mentor.

A special thanks to Barbara Correll, Director of the Learning Resources Department, Broward County Schools; The Recording Academy; Doug Smith, Domenic Grosso, and Roger Decker for their advice and continued support.

And finally, many thanks to all the recording artists, lyricists, and composers who inspired this collection.

Dedication

I dedicate this book to the three people in my life who have helped to mold and shape it into who I am today. I am indebted to my grandmother Helen Patchunka Wilson who passed in 2001. As a self-proclaimed artist, painter, and writer, she shared her creative talents with me which eventually led to the discovery of my own art expression.

To my mom, Helen Robinson, whose hard work and perseverance has not gone unnoticed. Her selfless, unconditional love is more precious to me than anything in the world.

To my one and only sister, Denise Robinson, who has been one of the important "pieces" of my life that I cherish. Thank you for your dedication and support in my endeavors.

About the Author

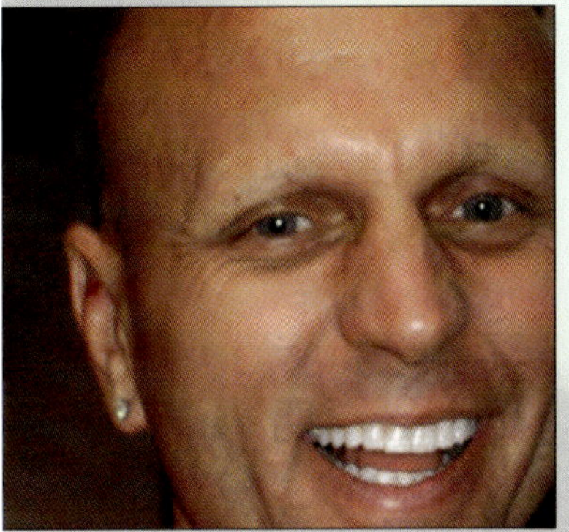

Pieces of Jimmy is a symbiosis of Robinson's innate appreciation of musical harmony and his personal agonies and triumphs. These 36 poetic expressions of love, hope, and celebration reflect the wonders of healing inspired by musical compositions and their artists.

A self-professed "late bloomer" and lyricist, Robinson perceives musical notes as pieces of himself. He urges his readers to strive and accept the pieces of themselves which they might otherwise discard or hide from. He is proof that acceptance gives way to a symphony within each one of us, making us whole and unique.

Pieces of Jimmy gives us a peek into how each of us can turn inward, pull our "pieces" together and make ourselves worthy of becoming friends to those around us—be they relatives, friends, or acquaintances.

Jimmy Robinson was born in 1964, and for a short period of his adult life, experienced a travailing homeless life. He currently lives with, and cares for his aging mother in Palm Beach County, Florida, where he writes enthusiastically.

Pieces of Jimmy is Robinson's first book, published by Jimmyland Corporation. Five more books are scheduled to be released in the near future.